MELANIE SPANSWICK

WOMEN COMPOSERS

A GRADED ANTHOLOGY
FOR PIANO

BOOK 1

GRADES 1–4

ED 23422

www.schott-music.com

Mainz · London · Madrid · Paris · New York · Tokyo · Beijing
© 2022 Schott Music GmbH & Co. KG, Mainz · Printed in Germany

ED 23422
ISMN 979-0-001-21351-6
ISBN 978-3-7957-2548-8

Contents

Elementary

Late Elementary

Early Intermediate

Musical Terms

Note values are given in the order American – British on their first mention within each section, then American terms alone thereafter.

whole note (semibreve)
half note (minim)
quarter note (crotchet)
eighth note (quaver)
sixteenth note (semiquaver)
thirty-second note (demisemiquaver)

Other terms follow British usage, for example:
bar (Br) = measure (Am)

Preface

Women Composers: A Graded Anthology for Piano is a three-book series featuring piano music by female composers. Intended as a progressive compendium of educational piano music, this series illustrates the rich and varied repertoire written by female composers from the Seventeenth century to the present day.

I have included a large variety of musical styles and genres, and you will find all types of music from Baroque dances and Classical sonata movements, through to jazz and swing numbers, as well as more adventurous Contemporary Classical music.

There are twenty-one works in Book 1 composed by twenty-one female composers, and they are arranged over three levels:

Elementary: Grades 1–2
Late Elementary: Grades 2–3
Early Intermediate: Grades 3–4

Each level might be considered broadly similar to the implied examination grades set by the various music exam boards in the UK. In this volume, a total of seven pieces are housed within each level. Several works composed by living, or Contemporary, composers have been written especially for this series.

Every piece is published alongside the composer's biography and performance notes for an optimal learning experience. Some fingerings, suggested metronome markings and pedalling have been added to most scores. I hope you enjoy this series and it will inspire a renewed interest in educational piano music composed by women.

Melanie Spanswick MMus (RCM) GRSM (Hons) DipRCM ARCM (PG)

www.melaniespanswick.com

Elisabetta de Gambarini
Minuet

from: *Six Sets of Lessons for the Harpsichord*, Op. 1,
Sonata No. 6 (second movement)

Elisabetta de Gambarini (1731–1765) was a British composer, singer, harpsichordist, conductor and an artist. Gambarini is thought to have studied with Francesco Geminiani, the composer of *The Enchanted Forest*. She was an accomplished musician, performing and composing for a variety of instruments, as well as for the voice.

Gambarini's career began as a singer, appearing in Handel oratorios. By 1761 her reputation was such that it allowed her to give a benefit concert performing her own music. She was the first British female composer to publish a collection of keyboard music: *Six Sets of Lessons for the Harpsichord*, Op. 1 (1748). She also published *Lessons for the Harpsichord Intermix'd with Italian and English Songs*, Op. 2 (1748), and *XII English & Italian Songs, for a German flute and Thorough Bass*, Op. 3 (1750).

Performance Notes

This attractive little *Minuet* appears in the *Sixth Lesson for Harpsichord*, Op. 1. Set in F major, the left hand provides a succinct accompaniment to the right-hand's melodic material. Aim to play through hands separately, noting any hand position changes, such as between bars 8–9 and 15–16 (right hand), and prepare to move swiftly from one position to the next.

Quarter notes (crotchets) would benefit from an elegant *non-legato* touch throughout, therefore, practice leaving each key, or note, cleanly at the very end of the beat, offering a short gap between notes. Eighth notes (quavers) should ideally be *legato*. Hand turns such as that in bar 1, beat 2 (from the C to Bb in the right hand), must be smooth, so try to support the fingers and hand with a flexible, relaxed wrist and arm before and during the larger movement required between the notes.

The suggested tempo is swift, but still allows for the three-in-a-bar lilt, necessary for this dance. Eighth notes, especially the triplets in bars 14 and 15, require a firm rhythmic pulse. Try to subdivide beats when counting, that is, count in eighth notes, placing every note, so that there is no sense of rushing or lingering.

Dynamically, the music could move from *piano* to *forte* between bars 1–8, dying away at bar 9, but ending powerfully at bar 16. The final ornament can be played as suggested at the bottom of the score, and notes within the chords in bars 7, 8 and 16 must sound altogether.

Minuet

Elisabetta de Gambarini
(1731–1765)

Allegretto ♩ = 126

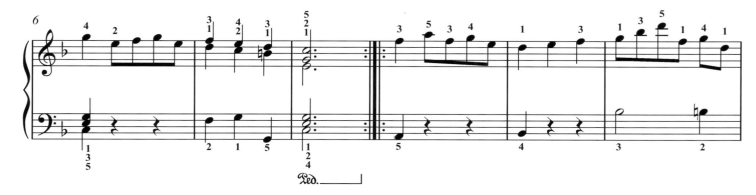

a)

Florence Ada Goodrich
Water Sprite

Florence Ada Goodrich (1850–1928) was an American composer and music educator. Goodrich mainly composed piano music for students of varying levels and abilities.

Collections of pieces include *Synthetic Series of Piano Pieces* (1907), *Preludes for Young Pianists* (published in 1938), *Suite for Small Hands* (1910), *Five Canonic Studies for the Piano* (first published in 1923), and *Four Little Pieces in C* (first published in 1915). *Water Sprite* was published in the year of Goodrich's death and it epitomizes her tonal, beautifully simplistic style, which is ideal for those learning to play; her works illustrate an understanding for the instrument, and many are imbued with wit and charm.

Performance Notes

Water Sprite is a light-hearted, impish depiction of this watery character. In the key of G major, Goodrich cleverly interplays the right and left hand; they play concurrently at bars 17–22.

Repeated note patterns are a feature, and the first three bars are a good example; a useful exercise might be to play all notes in each bar at the same time with the correct fingering, that is, as one chord. Next, play the first line, marking each bar by only playing its chord. This is an easy way to learn fingering and position changes. Once grasped, slowly play the note patterns as written, noting the octave higher marking in bar 1. Keep eighth notes (quavers) very even, both rhythmically and tonally, ensuring a pithy *staccato* articulation on beats 3 and 4 of bars 1, 2 and 3, and all similar. The half notes (minims) in bar 4 might be effective with a slight *tenuto* (or 'leaning'), as they form the end of the first phrase.

Bars 5–8 and 13–14 demand a smoother approach. Quarter notes (crotchets) in the left hand must run evenly onto beat 4 (played by the right hand), with a deeper touch on the first beat of bars 6, 8, and 14, phrasing off on beat 3, as marked. Bars 17–22 offer a different texture; the left-hand whole notes (semibreves) must be held for the entire bar and joined seamlessly to the following note in the next bar.

Observe the phrase marks in the right hand and aim to *crescendo* to bar 24, before repeating the opening, bringing the piece to a close at *Fine* (bar 16).

Water Sprite

Florence Ada Goodrich
(1850–1928)

Allegro ♩ = 152-168

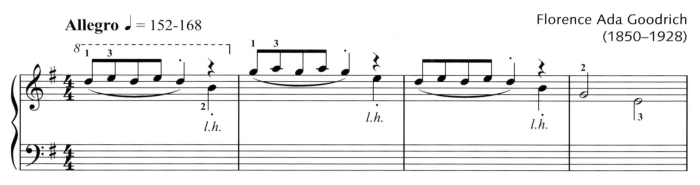

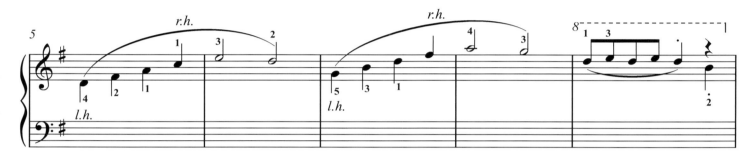

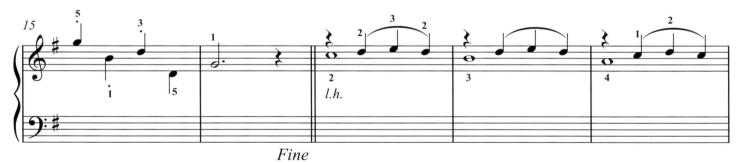

Fine

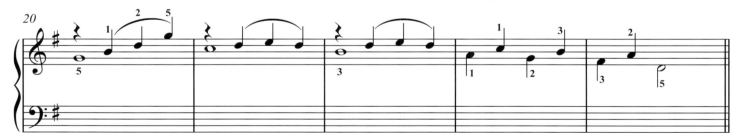

Da Capo al Fine

Narcisa Freixas
L'Ocell
from: *Piano Infantil*, Volume 1 (No. 8)

Spanish composer Narcisa Freixas (1859–1926) was a sculptor, painter and composer. Born in Catalonia, she studied painting and sculpting, later developing an interest in music, and subsequently studying the piano with Juan Bautista Pujol, who numbered Enrique Granados and Isaac Albéniz amongst his pupils.

Freixas published several collections of Catalan songs, nursery rhymes and piano pieces; the most popular of all her publications was *Children's Piano*, published in 1918 by the Muntañola publishing house. Her musical language was influenced by popular music, and many of her publications were illustrated by Pedro Torne Esquius' drawings. In 1909, Freixas founded the *Popular Musical Culture*, a pedagogical social project in Barcelona, teaching music, particularly singing and choral music, in schools to those who would not normally have the opportunity to study it.

Performance Notes

L'Ocell (The Bird) is the final piece in the *Piano Infantil* (Children's Piano), Volume 1. All set in the treble clef and in the key of A minor, its character is typical of a Spanish folk song. The piece begins in the implied key of A major with its added F♯s and G♯s, but switches to the minor at bar 9; it may be helpful to practice the scales of both A major and A minor when learning this work. The time signature §8 imbues the melody, which is in the right hand throughout, with a soaring, song-like demeanour, as might be expected from a bird. The left hand is purely accompaniment and the first note, an E dotted half note (dotted minim), needs a firm touch as indicated by the accent marking, despite the soft dynamics, because it must sound for four bars, providing a pedal note above which other musical lines flourish. Work at the two parts present in the left hand, separately, using the correct fingers. When playing them together, keep the upper line soft and *legato*.

The right-hand melody uses the same hand position for the first eight bars; place fingers over the five notes, ensuring similar weight is given to both black and white notes. The top note is usually the high point of the phrase, therefore gradually *crescendo* up to the B in bars 2 and 4, dying away afterwards, whilst still keeping the overall dynamic level soft.

Bars 9–14 offer a slightly different texture, the left-hand two-note chords move around, but still require complete *legato*, and the right hand must be smooth, with the exception of a scant breathing space at the end of the phrase at bars 11 and 13 (beat 1). Aim to give the ornament, or *acciaccatura*, in the penultimate bar (13), which is played an octave higher, a deeper touch.

L'Ocell

Narcisa Freixas
(1859–1926)

Vivo ♩. = 104-108

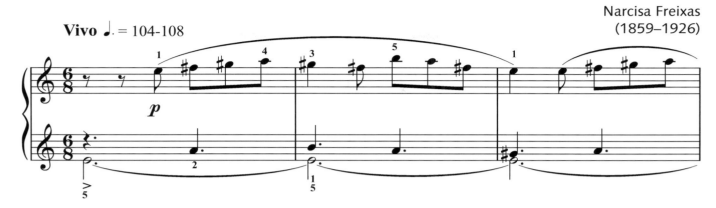

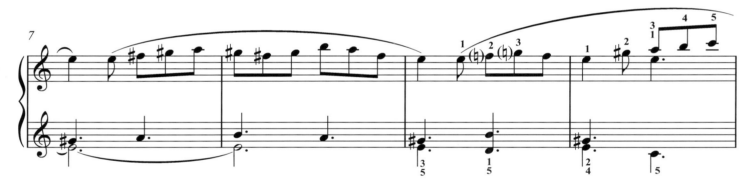

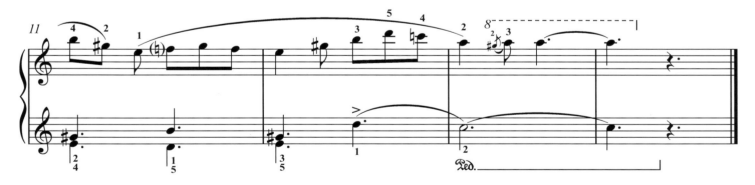

Felicitas Kukuck
The Boat
from: *Kleine Musikantenstücke* (No. 20)

Felicitas Kukuck (1914–2001) was a German composer and music educator. She undertook studies at the Berlin Musikhochschule majoring in flute and piano, and, until 1939, studied composition with Paul Hindemith, eventually becoming a private music teacher.

She was a member of several organisations including the artists organization GEDOK, and, in 1969, Kukuck founded the chamber choir Kammerchor Blankenese, which gave premieres of many of her works.

Kukuck was awarded the Biermann-Ratjen Medal in 1989 for her contributions to art and culture in Hamburg, and in 1994 she was honoured with the Johannes Brahms Medal for her contributions to the musical life of Hamburg. Kukuck is renowned for her vocal and choral music; the two most well-known works are the melody to the hymn *Manchmal kennen wir Gottes Willen* and the song *Es führt über den Main*.

Performance Notes

The Boat (original: Der Kahn) hails from the volume *Kleine Musikantenstücke* (Schott ED 4128) which was intended for voice (or narrator) and piano. This work feels akin to a song or a hymn, consisting of a melody and accompaniment. Whilst there is no key signature, E minor is indicated.

The left-hand chords at bars 1, 2, and 5–10, provide support for the lilting melody. Aim to join each one so that they form a *legato* accompaniment free from any breaks in the sound. To do this, play the first chord in bar 1 (an E and B) with a firm finger touch, so the keys are depressed together, and hold those notes until the very end of the beat. Keep the upper line of the left-hand chords *legato* as suggested by the fingering, releasing the fifth finger slightly before the next chord. To repeat the fifth finger on the E, gently lift the finger just a little, re-playing the key with a soft, slow depression.

The melody, in the right hand at bars 1–2 and 5–12 and in the left hand at bars 3–4, must consist of a rich timbre, singing out above the accompaniment. Decide which part of the phrase is most important, and which will need a softer colour. The opening theme might benefit from a nuance (or *tenuto*) on the F♯ (bar 1, beat 3), for example, dying away on the low B in bar 2. As the theme develops, from bars 5 to 9, a *crescendo* would add a sense of movement, before ending softly.

Try to move the left hand into position swiftly at bar 3 for its solo moment; keep the right-hand eighth notes (quavers) even and light here, and similarly, in the final two bars, the left-hand eighth notes must be soft, dying away at the end.

Einleiten (initiate or lead into) may refer to the changing timbre from the last two beats of bar 10 until the end, where the music moves into E major.

The Boat

Felicitas Kukuck
(1914–2001)

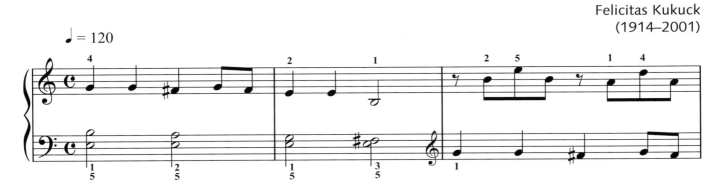

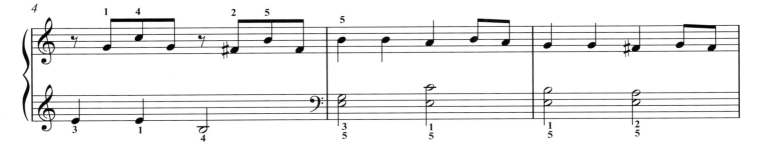

einleiten

Barbara Heller
Joker
from: *Flying Bird – Fliegender Vogel* (No. 5)

Barbara Heller (*1936) is a German composer and pianist, who studied music in Mannheim and Munich, graduating in 1957. After further studies in composition with Hans Vogt and Harald Genzmer, Heller received a scholarship to the Darmstädter Ferienkurse. From 1958 to 1962 she was a lecturer and piano teacher at the Mannheim Academy of Music. In 1986 Heller became a Board Member of the Institute for New Music and Music Education.

Heller was a founder member of Internationaler Arbeitskreis Frau und Musik e.V. (Women in Music Germany), and since 1978 she has dedicated herself to the works of forgotten female composers, researching, teaching and editing their music. She publishes the works of Fanny Hensel and of other contemporary female composers and, as a solo pianist and member of a number of chamber-music groups, she lends her support by performing their music.

In 1991, Heller participated in the foundation of the group *Bluna* producing tape compositions, sound installations, audio-visual exhibition projects and improvisations. As a composer she has produced a large body of works, including compositions for piano, harpsichord, orchestra, chamber ensembles, as well as film scores.

Performance Notes

Joker (original: Spaßvogel) comes from a collection of easy recital pieces for the piano entitled *Flying Bird* (Schott ED 22606). This sparely textured work focuses on various articulation. Set in G major, both hands utilise the treble clef. Plenty of slow practice might be required at the start in order to thoroughly assimilate the different touches, and Heller's phrase markings are also very precise.

When practicing the left-hand accompaniment figure at the opening, the hand position might feel a little unusual, that is, with the thumb on the F♯; the use of the thumb on a black note can be helpful, and in the case of the first two lines, it's one which precludes awkward hand position changes. This accompaniment pattern is given to the right hand at bars 11–22, and the use of the fifth finger on the F♯ also means the hand can remain in one position.

The melody, in the right hand at bars 1–10, needs a brighter sound and a fairly sprightly, detached *staccato* touch; even though a short and sharp articulation is necessary, be sure not to rush, 'placing' each beat, and therefore keeping a steady pulse.

A $\frac{3}{4}$-time signature gives the piece a dance-like quality, and one particular feature to be noted when practicing hands together, is the use of *staccato* markings at the ends of bars, which offers the breathing space needed to capture the 'witty' character. Strong dynamic contrasts will also greatly help to promote the necessary humour. Be sure to observe the *ritardando* (slowing down) in the final bars.

Joker

Barbara Heller
(*1936)

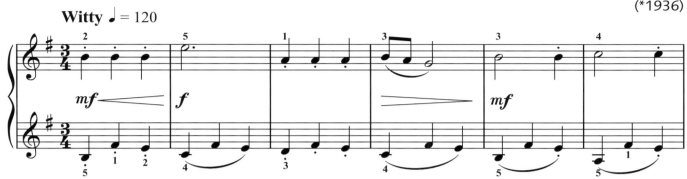

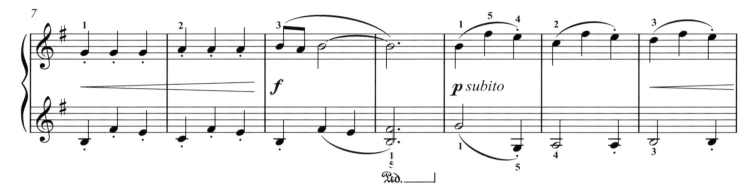

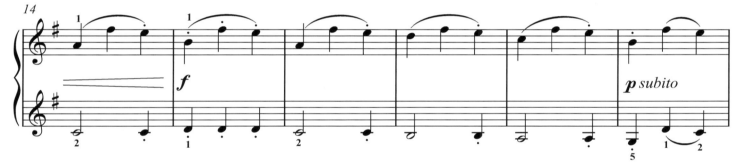

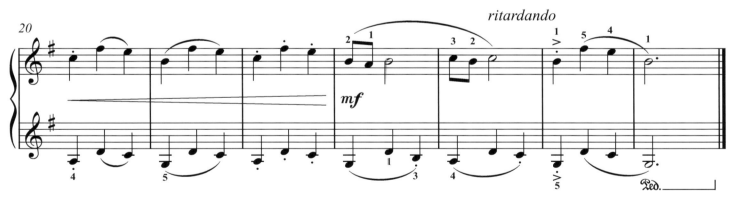

Melanie Spanswick
Mirage

Melanie Spanswick (*1969) is a British pianist, author, teacher and composer. Graduating from the Royal College of Music with a Master of Music degree in Performance Studies, she studied the piano with Patricia Carroll, Tatiana Sarkissova and John Lill.

As an educator, Spanswick has examined and adjudicated widely, and has given master classes, workshops and presentations throughout the UK and abroad, extensively touring the Far East. As a pianist, she has performed and broadcast worldwide, and has given recitals as a soloist, chamber musician and accompanist at many music festivals and major concert halls, and she has also released a solo album for *Opera Omnia* which was recorded at Wigmore Hall.

Spanswick has written and edited piano books for the international market, to critical acclaim. She is a regular contributor to Pianist Magazine and Piano Professional (EPTA), and is the author of the popular piano course, *Play it again: PIANO* (Schott ED 13935, ED 13945 and ED 14017). As a composer, she has written and published works for students and professionals, and her music has recently been performed and recorded in Japan, Germany, Serbia, Italy, Malaysia, Indonesia, and Singapore, as well as in the UK.

Performance Notes

Mirage, written in 2019, begins and ends with a soft, contemplative passage, synonymous with the title, and the addition of the sustaining pedal offers a resonance, in keeping with this character.

The first four bars, played in the upper part of the keyboard at the opening, and the last five bars, must be smooth, with the sound gradually subsiding; aim to observe the pauses in bars 4 and 15. Whilst this work appears to be key-signature free, the accidentals might indicate F minor.

A different texture prevails at bars 5–15. The rapid eighth note (quaver) figurations, in four-bar phrases, should ideally be very even, both tonally and rhythmically; counting aloud with an eighth note (quaver) or sixteenth note (semiquaver) beat will help in this respect. Aim to 'block out' (or play as a chord) each half note (minim) beat, sounding the notes altogether using the added fingerings throughout the piece, taking particular care at bars 14 and 15, where the hands are divided with a different note pattern. Keep the right hand flexible and relaxed when negotiating these bars, because the fingers and hand must move a little further than previously, especially in bar 14.

It can be helpful to practice without the sustaining pedal until note patterns are fluent and secure.

Mirage

Melanie Spanswick
(*1969)

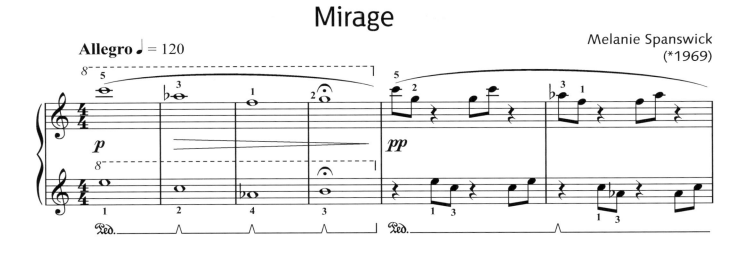

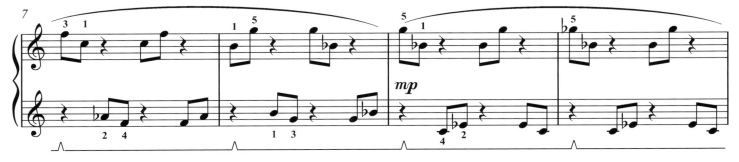

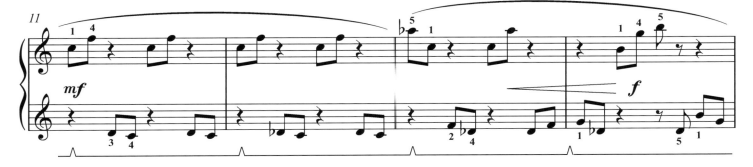

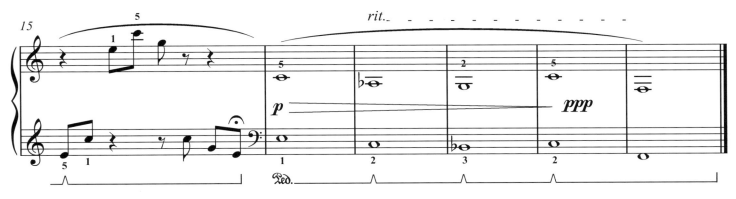

Rachael Forsyth
Soggy Shoes Blues

Rachael Forsyth (*1982) is a British musician, teacher and composer. She moved to London to study music in 2001 and graduated from Middlesex University in 2005 with a BA (Hons) in Music.

Following her graduation, Forsyth began working as an instrumental tutor and musician, playing in a wide range of styles from Classical music to jazz and ska. She's an avid saxophonist, all round woodwind player and pianist who is passionate about encouraging students of all ages to enjoy making music. An experienced session musician, Forsyth has also worked regularly in orchestral pits for various shows.

Forsyth began composing professionally in 2011. In 2012 she won a commission with the *Donne in Musica* foundation to tour Italy with one of her solo saxophone pieces and to discuss her life as a female composer. She works regularly with ensembles of all shapes and sizes, exam boards, and also enjoys publishing her own pieces.

Performance Notes

Soggy Shoes Blues was written in 2019. In the key of C major, there are plenty of 'blue notes' which contribute to the laid-back feel.

The eighth note (quaver) passages demand a 'Slow Blues Swing', that is, every pair of eighth notes must be articulated as a triplet; the first note of the eighth note pair, should ideally take the lion's share of the beat, and sound for the length of the first two eighth notes of the triplet, and the second must sound for the final eighth note of the triplet beat. When playing this rhythmic pattern, as in the melody at bars 1–3, give a slight 'push' or *tenuto* (a 'leaning') marking on the first beat, and a lighter touch to the second eighth note beat. This rhythmic pattern is a feature of this style and should ideally be employed for every pair of eighth notes.

Keep the whole notes (semibreves), half notes (minims), and all longer notes in the left hand held for their full length and place the left-hand quarter notes (crotchets) in bars 4–6 and 12 with a deep touch observing all accents and *tenuto* markings. Keep in mind the phrase markings, as they add to the jaunty style.

Coordination between hands might need attention at bars 8–11. The triplets in bars 5, 6 and 11 can be played as written, but, again, with a distinctly laid-back character. The final three bars should gradually slow down (as indicated). Place the chords in bar 12 firmly and drift off with the right-hand melodic material before sounding the last octave Cs softly, but short and detached.

Soggy Shoes Blues

Rachael Forsyth
(*1982)

Élisabeth Jacquet de La Guerre
Menuet
from: *Pièces de clavecin* – Suite No. 4 (fourth movement)

Élisabeth Jacquet de La Guerre (1665–1729) was a French composer and harpsichordist. A child prodigy, she was born in Paris to a musical family, receiving her initial musical training from her father. As a young girl, she performed a harpsichord recital for King Louis XIV, who became her patron. After her marriage in 1684 to Marin de La Guerre, she subsequently taught, composed and gave concerts both at home and throughout Paris.

Jacquet de La Guerre was one of the few renowned female composers of her time and she wrote in many different genres. Larger works include an opera-ballet, *Les jeux à l'honneur de la victoire* (1685, now lost), and a five-act opera, *Cephale et Procris* (performed in 1694). Jacquet de La Guerre's keyboard music is typical of the French style of this period; she wrote two books for solo keyboard, in 1687 and 1707, the latter of which is a collection of sonatas for harpsichord with an optional violin part. These volumes are apparently the first to be published by a woman.

Performance Notes

This elegant dance movement is taken from the *Pièces de Clavecin* (Pieces for Harpsichord) which was written in 1687. The piece includes many ornaments, which are synonymous with the French Baroque style. It might be beneficial to begin with separate hand practice, omitting the ornamentation at first, focusing on assimilating the fingerings and hand position changes.

In F major, a firm three-in-a-bar pulse is required; keep in mind short 'breathing' spaces which can be implemented at the end of each four-bar phrase, for example, between bars 4 and 5; this will assist in capturing the appropriate dance character expected of a Minuet. Quarter note (crotchet) beats can be played with a *non-legato* touch, that is, lifting fingers off the keys at the end of every quarter note beat. Eighth note (quaver) beats can remain *legato*. It may be helpful to observe a long-short-short articulation in bars containing three quarter note beats, promoting the Minuet style. In keeping with the French style, the performance practice *notes inégales* (unequal notes) might be appropriate for eighth note passages; the first note of an eighth note pair is dotted, and the second, articulated as a sixteenth note (semiquaver).

From bar 10 onwards, the left hand often contains two parts. Practice each musical line separately with the correct fingering, ensuring that the longer notes, such as the half notes and dotted half notes (minims and dotted minims), are held for their full value. When secure, add the ornaments (as suggested at the bottom of the score), ensuring fingers move smoothly across the keys; try to use a firm touch when practicing, lightening that touch when playing at speed. If the ornamentation feels overwhelming, play one or two ornaments per phrase, omitting the rest.

Aim to *crescendo* to bar 8, with a softer dynamic in bars 9–14. The reprise of the theme might be effective with a *mezzo-forte* rising to a *forte* in the final bar.

Menuet

Élisabeth Jacquet de La Guerre
(1665–1729)

Allegretto ♩ = 104-108

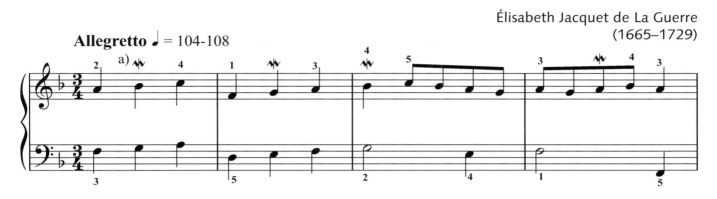

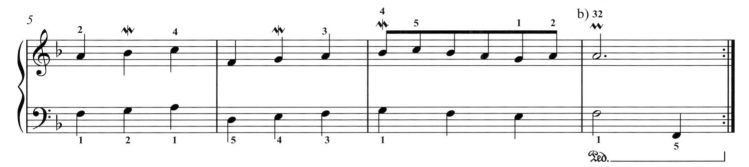

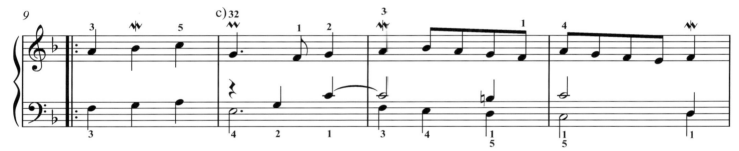

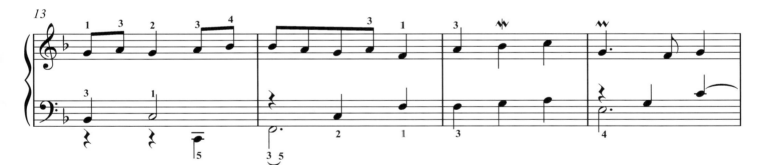

Marjory Kennedy-Fraser
A Harvest Reel
from: *Harvest Lilts*, Scots Suite, Volume 1 (No. 2)

Marjory Kennedy-Fraser (1857–1930) was a Scottish singer, folksong collector and editor, born to a musical family in Perth. She lived in Edinburgh and made a living as a music teacher and lecturer. Her father was her first teacher, and she completed her studies with Mathilde Marchesi in Milan and Paris.

Brought up on Scottish folk songs, Kennedy-Fraser developed a specific interest in Gaelic folk songs from the Hebrides and she began a personal project to record and transcribe the music from this region, recording the songs with a wax cylinder phonograph, and later arranging them for voice and piano, as well as for voice and harp. These songs were published in several volumes; *Songs of the Hebrides* (1909, 1917, and 1921), *From the Hebrides: Further Gleanings of Tale and Song* (1925), and *More Songs from the Hebrides* (1929).

She was awarded a CBE and an honorary degree of Doctor of Music from the University of Edinburgh in 1928. In 1930 she presented her archives of songs to the university library, and they have subsequently been re-recorded for the Sound Archives of the School of Scottish Studies.

Performance Notes

A 'Reel' is a traditional Scottish dance, which is notated in simple metre with either a $\frac{2}{2}$- or $\frac{4}{4}$-time signature, consisting largely of eighth note (quaver) movement with an accent on the first and third beats of the bar (in $\frac{4}{4}$ time).

In the key of G minor, this work is characterised by its sixteenth note (semiquaver) movement in the first eight bars, with the left hand imitating the right, and the 'tune' is that of a traditional Scottish folk song. The opening eight bars can be played precisely by counting each quarter note (crotchet) beat in sixteenth notes (semiquavers), taking care not to rush the final four eighth notes (quavers) in each of bars 1, 2, 3, 5, 6 and 7. At the end of bar 3, both hands will need to change positions, and this is also the case at bar 12 (beats 3–4).

A different character prevails at bars 9–16. Accentuate the *acciaccaturas* in the left hand at bar 9, keeping a steady pulse in order to effectively implement the right-hand triplet (on beat 2). Observe the accents on the chords at bars 11 and 15, becoming immediately softer during the two succeeding bars. The chords need a large, full sound; in order to play powerfully, with the hands in an out-stretched position required to play octaves and chords, the hands and wrists should ideally be flexible and relaxed, whilst employing necessary arm-weight.

After the repeat, the final five bars can die away with the *fermata*, or pause, slowing the tempo, drifting off into the distance.

A Harvest Reel

Marjory Kennedy-Fraser
(1857–1930)

Merrily ♩ = 116

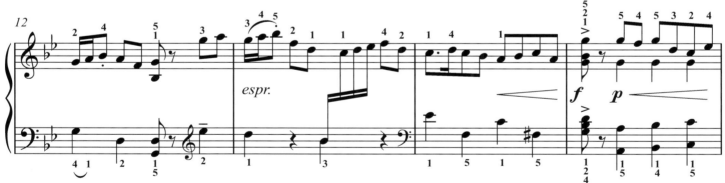

Hedwige Chrétien
Pierrot sautille
from: *Six petits préludes récréatifs* (No. 4)

Hedwige Chrétien (1859–1944) was a French composer and teacher. She studied with Ernest Guiraud at the Paris Conservatoire, winning first prizes in both harmony and fugue in 1881; in 1889, she became a professor at the Conservatoire. She also won prizes in both piano and composition at various competitions.

Chrétien composed around 150 works, including 50 songs, 50 piano pieces, two one-act comic operas, a ballet, and several chamber and orchestral works. She employed a Twentieth Century musical idiom, using ninth, eleventh and thirteenth chords, with chromatic melodies and frequent changes of metre and tonality, often modulating into remote keys.

Chrétien's fame extended beyond France to England and the USA. Some of her songs were translated and published in England, and her wind quintet was reprinted in the USA; the most extensive collection of her music is housed at the University of Michigan's Women Composers Collection.

Performance Notes

Set in the key of E minor and consisting of four-bar phrases, *Pierrot sautille* means 'Hopping Pierrot'; a lively Pierrot behaves as might be expected from this clown-like character.

A suggested tempo of a quarter note (crotchet) equals 100 beats per minute, moves this piece along nicely, and the *fermatas*, or pauses, at bars 8 and 32 would be effective if preceded by a slight *ritenuto*, or a slowing down, as indicated at bar 31, depicting this unpredictable, capricious personality.

Aim for a steady tempo; it might be worth counting four eighth notes (quavers) to each bar, and it may also help to learn the note patterns as chords (one chord per bar) in order to become comfortable with fingering and hand position changes; the right-hand part does occasionally move out of position, and quick movement will be necessary between bars such as 1 and 2, 5 and 6, and at bar 19.

The left-hand part, which is written in the treble clef throughout, must remain smooth and connected, offering a pedal-note effect to the right-hand melody. The majority of the eighth notes (quavers) in the right-hand part should ideally be short, sharp and very detached.

Be sure to observe the *tenuto* markings on the second beat of bars 2, 6, 10, 14, 18, 26 and 30. This slight 'leaning' into the note offers a brief moment of reflection. Always count precisely at bars 21–24; the upward *staccato* scale, split between the hands, is succeeded by quarter note rests before and after the two *staccato* quarter notes, E and B, possibly capturing a thoughtful Pierrot, before the free-spirited Pierrot returns in the final eight bars.

Pierrot sautille

Hedwige Chrétien
(1859–1944)

Allegretto ♩ = 100

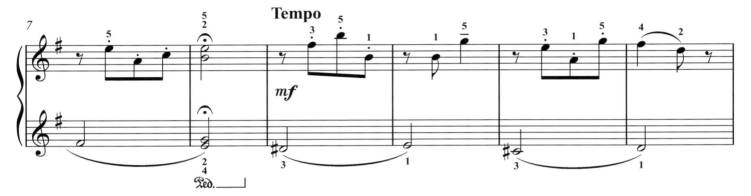

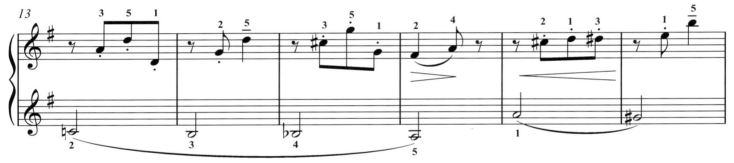

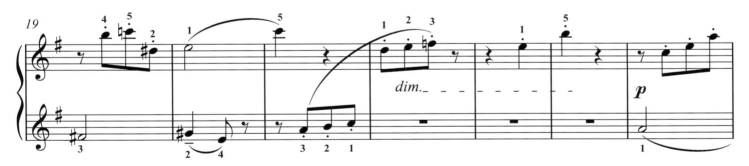

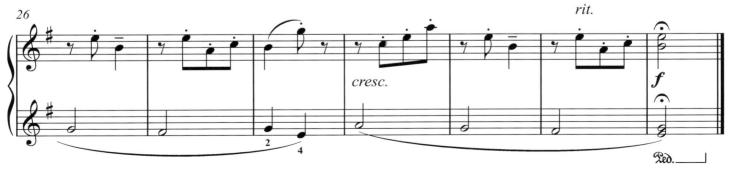

Gertrud Orff-Willert
Andante con moto
from: *Kleine Klavierstücke*, Book 1 (No. 6)

Gertrud Orff-Willert (1914–2000) was a German composer and collaborator in the foundation of the Orff School of Music for Children. After graduating from high school, she attended a private commercial school before devoting her life to music. Orff-Willert was the second wife of German composer Carl Orff, to whom she was married from 1939 to 1953.

Orff-Willert was involved in the development of the *Orff Schulwerk*, or the *Orff Approach*, which is a developmental approach used in music education. The *Orff Schulwerk* combines music, movement, drama, and speech into lessons. It was developed by Carl Orff and his colleague Gunild Keetman during the 1920s. Orff-Willert implemented this 'approach' in schools and worked extensively with special needs children. She composed and published four volumes of music for piano entitled *Small Piano Pieces (Kleine Klavierstücke)*. Her writing as a music therapy author includes: *The Orff music therapy. Active promotion in the development of the child* (1974) and *Key terms of Orff music therapy* (1984).

Performance Notes

The sixth piece of *Kleine Klavierstücke* (Small Piano Pieces) Book 1, this work was not only intended for children, but 'older players' too, and, according to the composer's notes, this particular piece should ideally be viewed as a dialogue with 'someone who was leaving', which explains the wistful character.

Both musical lines are written in the treble clef, and whilst a fairly slow tempo prevails (*Andante con moto*, or at a walking pace but with movement), a crucial component here is the need for a smooth, even touch throughout, as written: *ben legato*.

The left hand may need considerable work to acquire a truly *legato* line, but the suggested fingering will help, and if implemented, will enable fingers to move across the keys seamlessly from one chord change to the next. Further to this, try using a flexible, slightly rotational wrist motion, and give the first note of each bar (which is usually the lowest note) a deeper touch.

The right hand contains the melodic material and is notable for the copious articulation marks. The *tenuto* markings at the beginning are further enhanced by those at the top of the first phrase (bars 5 and 6). Aim to keep fingers almost glued to the keys, with the possible exception of ends of phrases; the finger-key connection combined with arm weight will help produce a rich sound when carrying longer notes, such as those at bars 13–16, with the fullest sound (perhaps a *mezzo-forte*) required on the A at the beginning of bars 17 and 24.

Andante con moto

Gertrud Orff-Willert
(1914–2000)

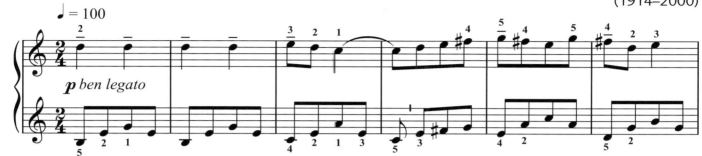

Ivana Loudová
The Sleeping Beauty
from: *Good Night Fairy-Tales,*
Ten small Instructional Compositions for Piano (No. 7)

Ivana Loudová (1941–2017) was a Czech composer. She studied composition at the Prague Conservatory with Miloslav Kabeláč, and the Academy of Music and Dramatic Arts with Emil Hlobil, later moving to Paris on a French Government Scholarship to study with Olivier Messiaen and Andrew Jolivet. Concurrently, she also undertook an internship at the Groupe de Recherches Musicales in Centre Bourdan.

Loudová has written for many genres including orchestral, chamber, choral and vocal music, and music for films and the stage, as well as music for children. She won several prizes in national and international competitions, including the Guido d'Arezzo International Polyphonic Competition in Italy in 1978, 1980 and 1984.

From 1992, she taught composition at the Academy of Music and Dramatic Arts in Prague, and she was a jury member at many competitions. Throughout her life she received a collection of awards, including the Ministry of Culture Award for Achievement in the Field of Music (2015). In 1996, she founded 'Studio N', a studio for Contemporary music.

Performance Notes

The Sleeping Beauty is an instructional composition from the collection *Good Night Fairy-Tales*, Book 1 (Schott P 2449). The dance character is present from the tempo marking; the jaunty three-beats-per-bar combined with the lilting nature of the left hand.

At bars 1–8 the left-hand quarter notes (crotchets) on the second and third beats should ideally be light, very short, and almost innocuous, allowing the important first beat of the bar to be 'placed' by the right-hand note, which is often *staccato*. This might possibly indicate the playful nature of the 'Sleeping Beauty'. Ensure the melody carefully adheres to the precise phrasing, with frequently short phrase marks and detached articulation, and keep a firm pulse until bar 16.

Chromaticism such as the E♭ (left hand, bar 3), and C♯ (left hand, bar 5) add colour, and would benefit from a richer nuance. This is especially true at bar 16, where the left hand moves into the treble clef to play a two-note chord (or dyad) with the right hand; observe the *sforzando* and *fermata* here.

The *Meno mosso, misterioso* demands a different timbre; the tone clusters should be balanced and must sound at the same moment. Over the period of four bars, a dramatic *fortissimo* is required, ending with a heart-stopping accented chord (at bar 20); could this be where 'Sleeping beauty' awakes? The sustaining pedal might be effective if used continuously here (as marked). As *Tempo I* is resumed, return to the assumed pulse and be sure to count the rest before the final chord!

The Sleeping Beauty

Ivana Loudová
(1941–2017)

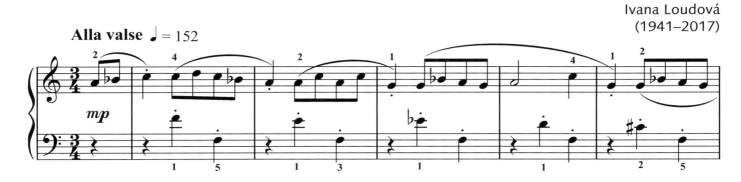

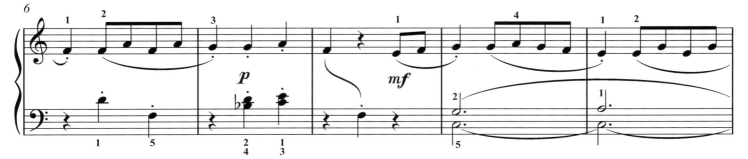

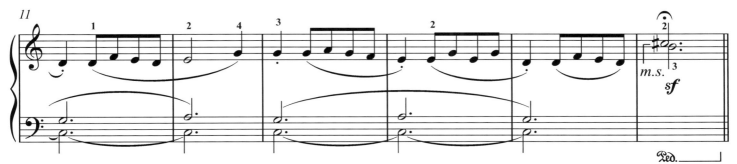

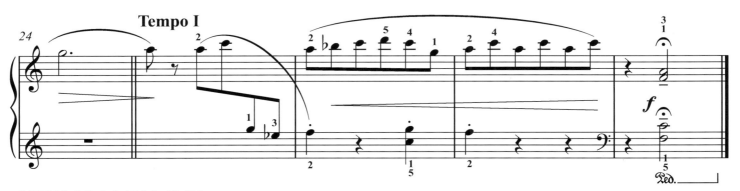

This page has been left blank to avoid unnecessary page turns.

Wendy Hiscocks
Fig and Fennel

Australian composer and pianist Wendy Hiscocks (*1963) was born in Wollongong and studied composition with Peter Sculthorpe at Sydney University. In 1988 she moved to London and has since received commissions and premières from around the world. Artist collaborations have included Piers Lane and Roy Howat (piano), Rachel Nicholls and Elizabeth Connell (soprano), Madeleine Mitchell & Philippa Mo (violin) and Michael Collins (clarinet). Venues range from the Aldeburgh Festival and Bangor New Music Festival (UK), Australian Festival of Chamber Music (composer-in-residence), Amadeus Festival (Geneva) to the Kusatsu International Summer Academy and Festival (Japan). Broadcasts have been aired on Radio Suisse Romande, France, ABC radio and TV, and BBC Radio 3, with a British Film Institute release of her music for the archival restoration of *Alice in Wonderland* (1903) creating something of a YouTube sensation, achieving over a million hits.

Her latest CD on Naxos performing the songs of Arthur Benjamin and Edgar Bainton indicates her specialist interest in Australian music, and she is currently Artistic Director of *Celebrating Australian Music* (CAM).

A recent new volume *Explorer* features twenty-seven piano duets for adventurous teachers and students and is published by Revolution Arts.

Performance Notes

This lively piece contains elements of both a 'rag' and a 'jig', as suggested by the composer: "*Fig and Fennel*, an unusual combination but it makes a delicious chutney and with a bit of imagination it can turn into a Fennel Rag and Fig Jig."

Written in 2019, *Fig and Fennel* is characterised by its humour, which calls for rhythmic precision. Start by tapping the right-hand rhythm on the piano lid and follow this by tapping the left-hand rhythmic pattern. When confident, tap both lines at the same time, and make sure you keep a strict pulse; either count aloud or use the metronome to help here, and begin slowly. Take note of the changing time signatures, from $\frac{2}{4}$ to $\frac{6}{8}$ and back again, and be sure to observe rests, particularly those at the ends of bars (such as at bars 14, 15, 21, 22 and 26), as well as all tied notes.

It might be easier to learn each hand separately; start by practicing *legato*, only adding the copious articulation markings, such as *staccato* and accents, when secure. The insistent accent markings will add the necessary swing, and a short, spikey *staccato* touch will capture the humorous, jocular feel.

Coordination between hands needs attention; the left-hand's accents on beat 2 of bars 1–8 must off-set the right-hand's on beat 1. Similarly, passagework at bars 21–23 requires precise hand coordination, and the final chord, with the right-hand an octave higher, can really ring out.

Fig and Fennel

Wendy Hiscocks
(*1963)

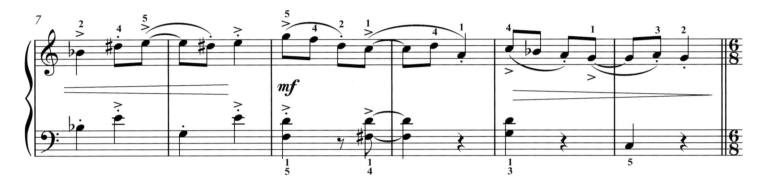

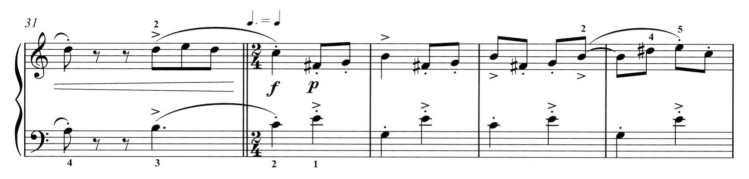

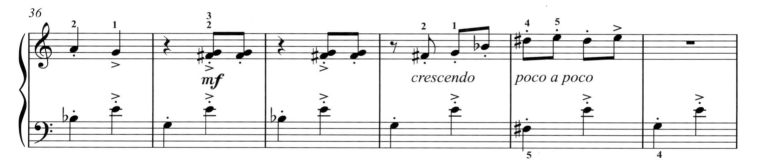

Vera Mohrs
Two Cats Playing
from: *Cat Songs* (No. 4)

German composer Vera Mohrs (*1984) was born near Cologne. She studied composition, song writing and singing at the Hanover University of Music, Drama and Media, and German philology at Leibniz University, also in Hanover.

Since 2005, Mohrs has been the singer and songwriter of the band *Vera's Kabinett*, performing over 250 concerts, and producing three recordings for the label Traumton Records, which is based in Berlin. The band have appeared on the SWR, SR and NDR radio stations.

From 2005 to 2008, Mohrs was the keyboard player for the band *Lichter*, playing over 100 concerts, including appearances at the Immergut-Festival, Populario-Festival, Reeperbahn-Festival, and Mamallapuram-Festival. Since the 2018-19 season, she has directed for the Schauspiel (drama) at the Staatsheater Nürnberg.
Vera Mohrs is a composer, arranger and an editor for Schott Music.

Performance Notes

Two Cats Playing is, according to the composer, a 'romp around the garden' for two 'fluffy friends'. This piece hails from a set of twelve charming pieces called *Cat Songs* (Schott ED 20372).

Built entirely from chord progressions, the technical demands of this work are such that the notes patterns must pass between the hands seamlessly, perhaps imitating the two feline friends. A useful exercise might be to 'block out' each bar slowly, or play certain note patterns within each bar altogether, so that chord positions and fingerings become clear. This will work if each half bar is 'blocked' or played together; the following example illustrates bars 1–2.

Once the piece has been worked at using this exercise, practice as written, and keep the Es in the right and left hands (bars 1–4) light, with focused attention on the strong beats, which feature the changing harmonies and the melodic interest.

Try to practice with a firm touch when playing at slower speeds; this will help develop evenness coupled with a secure rhythmic grasp. It can help to count out loud when placing each eighth note (quaver) beat. As speed is added, lighten the touch and, hopefully, fingers should run across the keys smoothly. Two-note slurs play an important role; to play them fluently, depress the first note, holding it down for the full length of that note, rolling onto the second note, joining seamlessly, lifting off the key cleanly after the second note has been played. It may be necessary to 'overlap' the two notes just for a millisecond for a truely smooth join.

Mezzo-piano might be the only suggested dynamic marking, but more intensity will be required at bars 5–10 and 16–20. Observe the accent markings on the chords at bars 10 and 20, and ensure a substantial pause at bar 10, where the cats enjoy a moments rest!

Two Cats Playing

Vera Mohrs
(*1984)

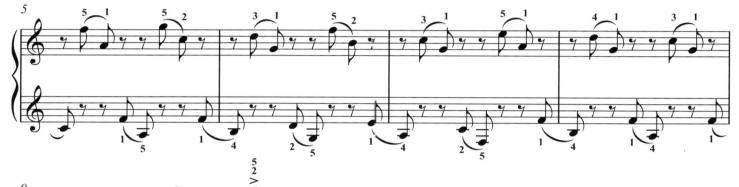

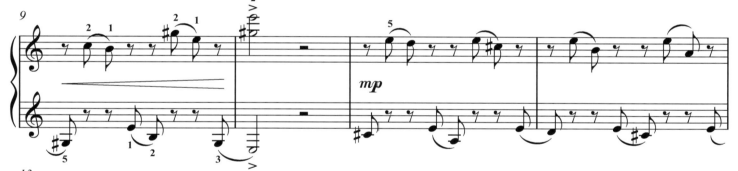

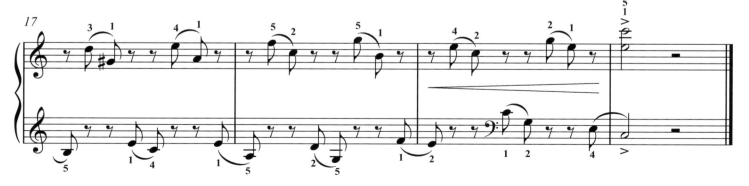

Anna Bon
Andante
from: *Six Harpsichord Sonatas*, Op. 2 (No. 2)

Italian composer and singer Anna Bon di Venezia or Anna Bon (1738 – after 1767) studied at the Ospedale della Pietà in Venice from the age of four, moving with her parents, who were both musicians, to the Bayreuth-based court of Princess Wilhelmine of Prussia in 1755. At the court, Bon assumed the position of 'Chamber music virtuosa'. Her first published works, *Six Chamber Sonatas for flute and continuo*, Op. 1 (1756) and *Six Sonatas for harpsichord*, Op. 2 (1757), were written when she was still a teenager.

After Princess Wilhelmine's death in 1758, the Bon family returned to touring, and Anna Bon's final set of works were published; *Six Divertimenti (Trio Sonatas) for two flutes and continuo*, Op. 3 (1759). Bon joined her parents in 1762, for further employment at the court of Prince Nicolaus of Esterházy in Eisenstadt. By 1767, she had married an Italian singer settling in Hildburghausen, Thuringia, after which she disappeared from musical history.

Performance Notes

This expressive piece, in G minor, which forms the second movement of *Sonata No. 2* for harpsichord, is akin to an aria, with its mellifluous melodic line which is predominantly in the right-hand part. Each hand should ideally be practiced separately because both contain significant material.

As this movement should be performed at a fairly stately tempo, and it exudes a *cantabile* musical line, a *legato* touch may be preferable, despite being written in the Baroque period. As a general rule, eighth notes (quavers) and quarter notes (crotchets) moving by step are smooth whilst those moving by intervals, are detached. Sixteenth notes (semiquavers) are best played *legato*. Ensure longer notes, such as the half note (minim) Gs, in bar 1 (left hand) and bar 2 (right hand) are held for their full value. Place the opening eighth notes, which pass between the hands, steadily and rhythmically, setting a firm pulse.

Non-harmony notes, such as added C♯s in bars 4 and 6, will colour each phrase as the music passes through several keys (for example, D minor at bars 5–7, and C minor at bars 14–15). The sequence at bars 12–17 might be effective with a gradual *crescendo*, returning to a softer dynamic at bar 20.

At bars 8–10, the left hand will need to be flexible and loose in order to negotiate the two parts; work at each part alone, with the correct fingering, ensuring that the lower part is even rhythmically, despite the awkward placing of the fourth and fifth fingers. Similarly, in the right hand, keep the hand relaxed and move swiftly into place between the two-part material at bars 28–31. The last three bars are much slower; aim to highlight the top line of the chords in the right hand, and the sustaining pedal may add resonance here, too.

Andante

Anna Bon
(1738–after 1767)

Maria Szymanowska
Mazurka
from: *25 Mazurkas* (No. 14)

Maria Szymanowska (1789–1831) was a Polish composer and pianist. Born in Warsaw, she was one of the leading female virtuoso pianists of the Nineteenth Century. She gave her first public recitals in Warsaw and Paris in 1810 and toured extensively throughout Europe. Szymanowska was one of the first pianists to perform from memory and she composed around 100 piano pieces, as well as songs and some chamber music.

Stylistically, the music is typically of Polish sentiment and might be described as early Romantic, of the *stile brilliant* genre, with an output consisting of dances, mazurkas, nocturnes, études and polonaises. As a concert pianist of virtuoso calibre, Szymanowska was able to expand and develop her technical capabilities as a composer, in a similar manner to that of her fellow Pole, Frédéric Chopin, whose own style was clearly influenced, in some respects, by that of Szymanowska. She played an important role in the early development of the virtuoso composer-pianist phenomena.

Performance Notes

On first inspection, this *Mazurka* which hails from a set of 25 mazurkas, may look complicated, but it lies conveniently under the hands. A *Mazurka* is a traditional Polish dance, and, in this work, the right hand contains the melodic material, requiring a deeper, brighter sound, and the left hand must accompany with a softer touch.

The key, E♭ major, has a warm, rich colour, and the key-signature might swiftly be assimilated by practicing the scale and arpeggio. The first half of this piece should ideally be played at fairly brisk speed (the *Allegretto* marking is a suggestion), with a powerful, dramatic opening four bars; bars 4–8 might be softer and lighter (*mezzo-piano* or *piano*). Bars 9–12 could be a little slower, but played with a *forte* dynamic marking, highlighting the bold material.

Despite the necessity for some *rubato* (or taking time), aim to keep the melodic material rhythmical. Observe articulation marks, for example, at bars 2, 3, 9, 10, 13 and 14, where *marcato* markings need a firmer touch, adding nuance and character to the phrases, appropriate for this dance. A flexible wrist will be necessary to circumnavigate the note patterns in the right-hand melody at bars 4, 9, 10, 13 and 14.

The left-hand chords may be worked at slowly; focus on the position changes from bar to bar, aiming to balance fingers on the notes, depressing them concurrently, so chords sound altogether. Observe the ornament in the final bar, which has been written out at the foot of the score and keep the *acciaccaturas* in bars 13 and 14 light.

Mazurka

Maria Szymanowska
(1789–1831)

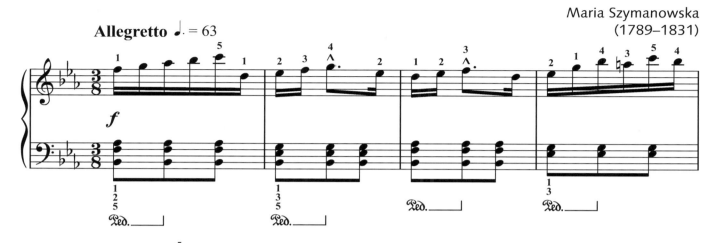

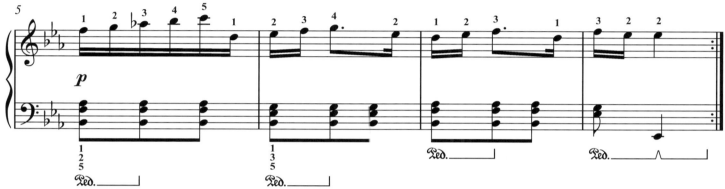

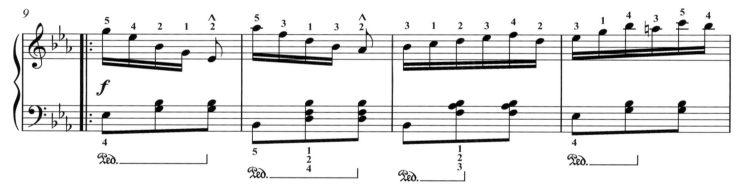

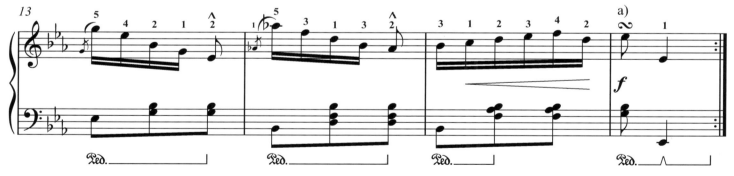

a)

Elfrida Andrée
Allegro moderato
from: *Fem smärre tonbilder*, Op. 7 (No. 3)

Swedish composer, conductor and organist Elfrida Andrée (1841–1929) was born in Visby, and initially taught by her father. She studied composition with Ludvig Norman at the educational institution of the Royal Swedish Academy of Music, and also with Niels Wilhelm Gade. Andrée was the first woman to graduate as an organist and to become a cathedral organist; she was elected organist of Gothenburg Cathedral in 1867, a job she kept until her death.

Andrée was known equally well in her native country as a pioneer advocate for the rights of women. She was the younger daughter of Andreas Andrée, a progressive politician, and her elder sister was the acclaimed opera singer Fredrika Stenhammar. She wrote music for many different genres including two organ symphonies, an opera (*Fritiofs saga*), two orchestral symphonies, a piano quartet and piano quintet, two Swedish masses, as well as chamber and instrumental works, and songs. Andrée was conductor of the 'Workers Institute Concerts', establishing her reputation as the first Swedish woman to conduct a symphony orchestra.

Elfrida Andrée's work as a female pioneer was recognised when she was elected as a member of the Royal Swedish Academy of Music in 1879.

Performance Notes

Allegro moderato, which is in the key of G minor, is the third work from a set called *Fem smärre tonbilder*, Op. 7 (Five Little Sound Pictures). Whilst the pulse is quite swift, there is ample time to phrase the melodic material, and distinguish between the various articulation marks. Rests, which are prevalent in both hands, should ideally be fully observed, therefore try to count aloud 'placing' every eighth note (quaver) beat.

The *staccato* touch can be gentle and light as opposed to short and sharp; this is because the character is generally expressive, with soft dynamics and a slightly mysterious semblance. Practice all chords in the left hand separately, taking care to depress the notes within them altogether – it can help to play with a heavier touch at first, and when the fingers and hand have gauged the necessary balance, lighten that touch.

The right-hand melody occasionally features two parts, as at bars 9 and 13; here, place the fifth finger firmly on the top note (F), and keep depressed until the end of the bar, whilst the lower part requires an independent *staccato* touch. This note pattern also occurs in the left hand at bar 15.

The *ritenuto* at bars 15–16 allows for a natural pause; take note of the accent on the D in the right hand at bar 16. *Acciaccaturas*, or grace notes, at bars 8 and 24 can be very light, with the finger merely skimming over the key, and try ensuring fairly soft dynamics throughout, with the exception of bars 9–10.

Allegro moderato

Elfrida Andrée
(1841–1929)

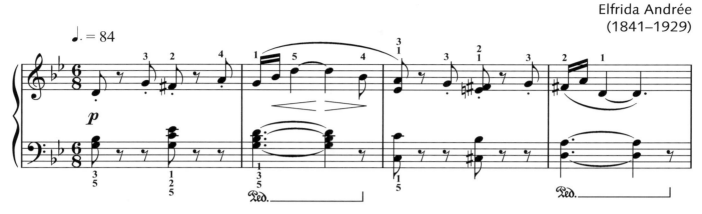

Agathe Backer Grøndahl
Song of Youth
from: *Fantasistykker*, Op. 45 (No. 1)

Agathe Backer Grøndahl (1847–1907) was a Norwegian composer and pianist. She was a piano student of Theodor Kullak and she studied composition under Richard Wüerst at the Akademie der Tonkunst in Berlin.

Backer Grøndahl made her debut as a pianist in 1867, performing with the Philharmonic Society, with Edvard Grieg as conductor, and in the same year she played at the Gewandhaus in Leipzig, after which she studied with Franz Liszt in Weimar in 1873. She also studied with Hans von Bulow in Florence in 1871. After marrying celebrated singing teacher, Herr Grøndahl of Christiana, Backer Grøndahl enjoyed an outstanding career as a pianist, giving many recitals and concerts in Nordic countries, as well as in London and Paris.

Backer Grøndahl was a renowned piano teacher. As a composer, her output consists mostly of piano pieces and songs, and she wrote over 400 works. She was a prominent figure on the Norwegian musical scene, and her style largely draws on the pianistic ideas of the Romantic period.

Performance Notes

Song of Youth (or *Ungdomssang*) is the first piece in a set called *Fantasistykker* (Fantasy Pieces), Op. 45. In F major, the *Tranquillo* tempo marking should be thoroughly heeded; this work feels calm and tranquil, generally requiring soft dynamics, but yet the pulse does move at a pace. Practice hands separately at first, in order to decide which hand will play which note. You may prefer to distribute notes differently to that marked on the score, and that is entirely possible here, with the left hand taking a larger proportion of the notes.

The melody, in the right-hand part and always at the top of the texture, must sing sweetly, as indicated by the *dolce* markings, and, as phrasing has been carefully marked, a *legato* line is paramount. The fingering has been written to accommodate a smooth melodic line; aim to play this top line through alone, using the suggested fingering, so that an expressive, rich and velvety tone ensues, even when *pianissimo*. It can help to 'skim' across the keys, avoiding any jerkiness. Next, add the lower notes, softly, joining as much of the texture as possible with the fingers, only employing the sustaining pedal when secure. It may be beneficial to change the sustaining pedal even more frequently than that marked, to avoid smudging harmonies.

Set in four bar phrases, chromatic chords abound and would benefit from extra colour and nuance; experiment with the chords in bar 1, beat 3, highlighting the B natural and G♯. And similarly, spotlight the chord progressions at bar 11, beat 3, and the D♭ at beat 2 in the penultimate bar.

Song of Youth

Agathe Backer Grøndahl
(1847–1907)

Ethel Smyth
Minuet
from: *Piano Suite* (third movement)

British composer and writer Ethel Smyth (1858–1944) was a prolific composer and member of the women's suffrage movement. Born in Kent to a military family, against her father's wishes Smyth decided to pursue a musical career, studying at the Leipzig Conservatory in Germany with Carl Reinecke, Louis Mass and Salomon Jadassohn. Further to her studies, she undertook harmony and counterpoint lessons with Heinrich von Herzogenberg and, whilst in Germany, met many of the most significant composers of the period, including Johannes Brahms, Antonín Dvořák, Clara Schumann and Pyotr Ilyich Tchaikovsky.

Smyth lived and worked in several European countries, before returning to the UK in 1890. Her output includes orchestral, chamber, instrumental and choral music, six operas and a ballet. She also wrote several books and copious articles. The *Mass in D*, *Concerto for Violin and Orchestra* and the opera *The Wreckers* are amongst her most popular works. Smyth worked tirelessly to secure performances of her works, and she was the first woman to have an opera produced at the Metropolitan Opera House in New York. She was made a Dame Commander of the Order of the British Empire (DBE) in 1922, becoming the first female composer to be awarded a damehood.

Performance Notes

This *Minuet* might not be considered 'typical' of the expected three-in-a-bar dance, with its compound duple time signature and two-part counterpoint, but, in this respect, it is much more similar to a two-part invention.

In E major, it may be helpful to play the scale and arpeggio before learning commences, in order to familiarize with the four sharps in the key signature. Each hand will require plenty of slow practice as both parts are independent.

As always in this style, a firm rhythmic pulse is imperative. Try keeping time using a sixteenth note (semiquaver) beat; counting out loud can be helpful. This will allow careful 'placement' of the thirty-second notes (demisemiquavers) which occur frequently, as at bar 3 (right hand) and bar 6 (left hand). It's crucial that these short note values don't rush or linger; if the short notes are placed rhythmically, the overall pulse should remain precise.

The four-bar phrase structure may benefit from a 'lift' at the end of each phrase proffering the dance character, and some *non-legato* articulation in the left-hand part might be effective, for example in the eighth notes (quavers) on the second beat of bars 8 and 16.

Devoid of dynamics, this offers the freedom to explore various options; begin softly, building the first four bars, so that when similar thematic material (to the opening) returns at bar 5, assume a *mezzo-piano* dynamic, before implementing a *crescendo* to bar 8. In the second half, start softly *(mp)*, moving to a *forte* *(f)* at bar 13, before dying away after the top E on the second beat of bar 15.

Minuet

Ethel Smyth
(1858–1944)

Andante ♩. = 48

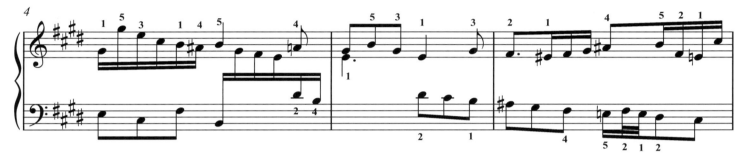

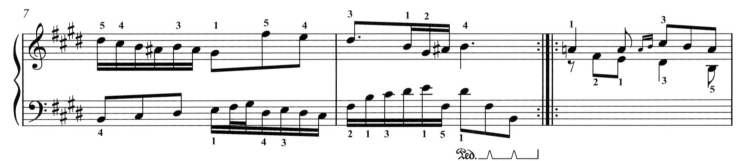

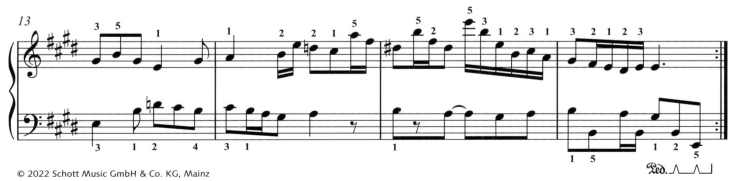

45

Frère Jacques

Mélanie Bonis
(1858–1937)

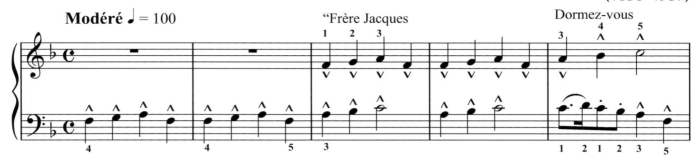

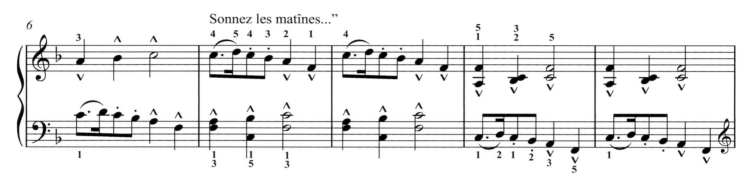

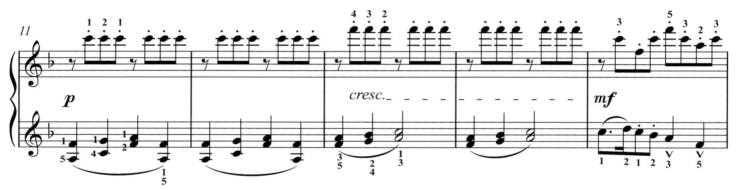

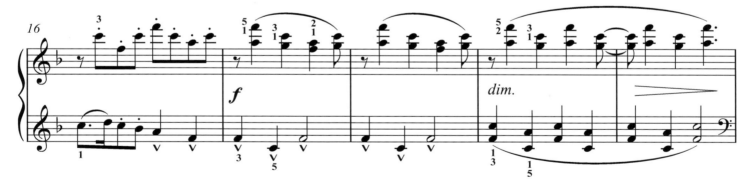

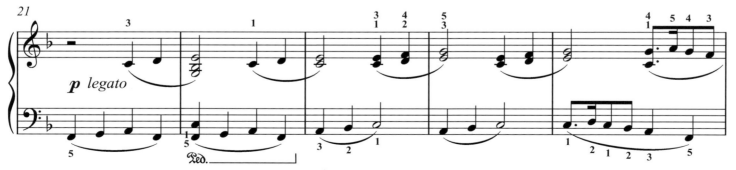

Un peu plus lent

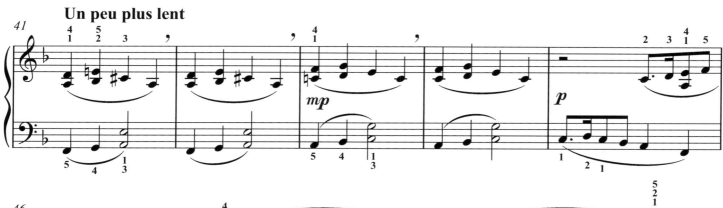

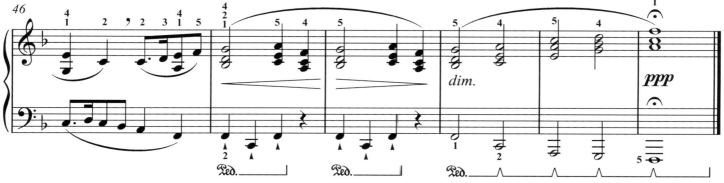

Mélanie Bonis
Frère Jacques
from: *Scènes enfantines*, Op. 92 (No. 6)

Mélanie Bonis (1858–1937), known as Mel-Bonis, was a French composer. Born in Paris, she attended the Paris Conservatoire, where she studied alongside fellow students Claude Debussy and Gabriel Pierné. Her teachers included Cesar Franck, Ernest Guiraud and Auguste Bazille.

Whilst a student, Bonis met Amédée Landély Hettich, a student, poet and singer. Her parents disapproved of the match and, in 1883, arranged a marriage to businessman Albert Domange. Bonis had three children with Domange and gave up composition for over ten years.

When Bonis met Hettich again, in the 1890s, their affair resumed, leading to the birth of their child, Madeleine, who was put into the care of her chambermaid. Hettich encouraged Bonis to return to composition, introducing her to publisher Editions Alphonse Leduc, and she also became a member of the Société des compositeurs de musique.

Bonis wrote more than 300 pieces, most of which were published, and these include works for solo piano and organ, piano duet and piano works for children, chamber music, songs, choral music, a mass, and works for orchestra.

Performance Notes

The traditional tune *Frère Jacques* has been transformed into a charming little piece intended for children. It's the sixth piece in a set called *Scènes enfantines*, Op. 92.

The famous melody appears in many guises throughout the piece, and on each occasion, it will be necessary to play it with a deeper touch, keeping the surrounding accompanying material soft.

The left hand requires a specific articulation at the opening, as each note appears with a *marcato* ('marked') touch; separate every note with a distinct *non-legato* touch coupled with a short accent. This can be mimicked in the right hand at bars 3–6, where there is a canonic entry, as might be expected from such a piece, which can be sung as a round (or with many entries). The dotted eighth note (quaver) pattern at bar 5 and bar 6 in the left hand, and at bar 7 and bar 8, in the right, should ideally be clear and crisp with precise rhythmic enunciation. With this in mind, it may be useful to count in sixteenth notes (semiquavers) throughout, taking care to 'place' the shorter notes without rushing.

The *staccato* articulation in the right-hand part at bars 11–16 can be lighter, but bars 17–20 might need attention regarding coordination; practice the right-hand figurations as a chord, 'blocking out' at first. From this point onwards, a *legato* touch is mostly required. Incisive chords at bars 27–29 in the right hand demand sonority. The music crescendos up until bars 37–38, after which there is a gradual dying away, especially the *Un peu plus lent* – which signifies a slower tempo.

Samantha Ward
Rockin' Fingers

British pianist Samantha Ward (*1982) has performed extensively around the UK, China, Japan, Germany, Italy, France, Greece and Macau, making her London debut at Wigmore Hall in 2007. Ward was awarded a fellowship from the Guildhall School of Music and Drama in 2007/8, where she studied with Joan Havill. She previously studied with Leslie Riskowitz and Alicja Fiderkiewicz.

In August 2013, Ward founded PIANO WEEK, an international festival and summer school. At four consecutive years of the festival, Ward joined forces with Stephen Kovacevich for the closing recitals and in August 2019, she performed alongside internationally acclaimed Australian pianist Leslie Howard, as well as with her husband, fellow pianist and co-director of PIANO WEEK, Maciej Raginia. This festival continues to tour internationally alongside its UK residencies, to China, Italy and Japan.

In 2018, Ward toured Asia, which included giving master classes, seminars (for Schott Music Publishers) and performances in Macau, Malaysia, Indonesia, China and Singapore. She was also a jury member alongside Raginia at the Hong Kong Youth Piano Competition. 2019 saw the release of her album with SOMM recordings; two piano concerti by Dora Bright with the Royal Liverpool Philharmonic Orchestra under Charles Peebles.

Performance Notes

This perky piece, written in 2019, is fun to play and really rocks! The left hand needs a firm quarter note (crotchet) pulse as it negotiates the twelve-bar-blues pattern. The twelve-bar-blues is a structure which uses a repeated twelve bar chord pattern, featuring just three chords; the tonic, subdominant and dominant chords in the key of the piece. These chords appear in a specific order every time the twelve bars are repeated. Go through the left-hand part and try to spot the chords, and the chord pattern which they form. As indicated, keep quarter notes *non-legato*, only lifting fingers off the keys just before the next note is played. A deep touch works well for this type of accompaniment encapsulating the bright and breezy character.

The right-hand part, which contains the melodic material, features 'swung' eighth notes (quavers). To achieve this laid-back feel, each pair of eighth notes must be played as a triplet, so that the first eighth note takes the lion's share of the beat (or the value of the first two eighth notes) and the last note in the triplet, takes the final beat. When practicing the right hand, try counting each eighth note pair to a triplet beat, and give the first eighth note a slight 'push' or firmer touch, whereas the second can be played lightly.

The *acciaccaturas* are the 'blue notes', providing the appropriate nuance; give them time to sound and 'clash' against the eighth note pairs which follow. The *tremolo* (a 'shake') in the right hand at bar 12, will need slow practice; rotate the hand and wrist as the fingers play firmly into the key bed, and lighten the touch as speed is added.

Observe the *forte* marking at bar 23, after which the music gradually becomes softer with a *ritardando* in the final two bars.

Rockin' Fingers

Samantha Ward
(*1982)

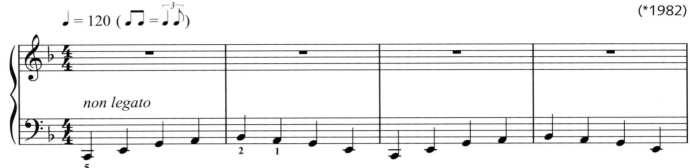

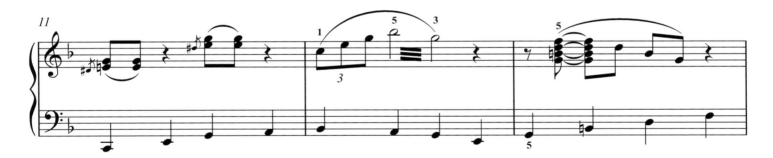